HOW IT HAPPENS
at the Post Office

By Dawn Frederick
Photographs by Bob and Diane Wolfe

CLARA
HOUSE
BOOKS

Minneapolis

The publisher would like to thank the United States Postal Service and its employees for their generous help with this book.

Clara House Books
The Oliver Press, Inc.
Charlotte Square
5707 West 36th Street
Minneapolis, MN 55416-2510

Library of Congress Cataloging-in-Publication Data
Frederick, Dawn, 1975-
    How it happens at the post office / by Dawn Frederick ; photographs by Bob and Diane Wolfe.
        p. cm. — (How it happens ; 3)
    Summary: Photographs and text describe how the United States Postal Service collects, processes, and delivers mail.
    ISBN 1-881508-92-7 (lib. bdg.)
    1. United States Postal Service—History—Juvenile literature. 2. Postal service—United States—History—Juvenile literature. [1. Postal service.] I. Wolfe, Robert L., ill. II. Wolfe, Diane, ill. III. Title. IV. Series.

HE6371 .F736 2002
383'.4973—dc21

                                                                    2001052974

ISBN 1-881508-92-7
Printed in the United States of America
08 07 06 05 04 03 02   8 7 6 5 4 3 2 1

The United States Postal Service delivers more than 200 billion pieces of mail every year. It carries more mail to more people over a larger area than the mail service of any other country! With so much mail traveling to so many different places, how can the letter you write today reach the right person in the right city just a few days later? This book will guide you step by step through the efficient system that collects, sorts, and delivers all types of mail—and allows you to communicate with friends and family anywhere in the world.

Collection

What happens after you drop a letter in the mailbox? Each day (except Sundays), mail carriers collect mail from homes, from businesses, and from public mailboxes like the one shown here. They take all the mail to the local post office.

Incoming Mail

At the large downtown post office shown here, postal workers unload the mail from trucks.

A machine called a **hamper dumper** picks up the big hampers (containers) full of mail and tips them forward. The mail falls out onto a **conveyor belt**, a moving platform that carries the mail with it as it moves.

Separating Letters

Postal workers sort through the mail and take out the packages, bundles, or unusually large or thick envelopes. These items are set aside, because they need to be handled by special machines. The conveyor belt carries all the normal-sized letters on to the next step of the process.

STAMP PRIORITY
CLEARANCE TIME
FOR EAGLE
TO ANNEX

1940

How do you handle
Global Priority Mail?

9

The letters are dumped into a machine called a **flat extractor**, which makes sure there are no remaining packages, bundles, or thick envelopes. A conveyor belt carries all the mail under the large, round roller shown below. There is not much space underneath the roller, so any thicker piece of mail can't fit. The thick pieces of mail are swept to one side, onto another conveyor belt that takes them to machines that can process them.

Facing and Cancelling

Postal workers load the normal-sized letters into a machine called an **Advanced Facer/Canceller** (AFCS). Each machine can handle 30,000 letters in an hour! The AFCS makes sure that all the letters are facing the same way, with the stamp in the upper right-hand corner. It is able to do this because postage stamps have a chemical called phosphorus in them. The machine senses the phosphorus on a corner of the letter and turns the letter so that corner is the upper right.

Postmark

Charlotte L.
7 E. Hennepin Ave.
Mpls. MN 55401

MINNEAPOLIS
PM
23 APR
2001

THE ABILITY TO WRITE • A ROOT OF DEMOCRACY
USA 1¢

CALIFORNIA GOLD RUSH 1849
USA 33

Uncle Steve
5707 West 36th St.
Minneapolis, MN 55416

55416+2510

Next, the AFCS cancels the stamp on the front side of each letter. When a stamp is cancelled, it is marked with a special pattern that proves the letter has passed through the post office. This pattern, called a **postmark**, shows the date of the cancellation and the location of the post office (which can be helpful if you want to know what day a letter was mailed or where it came from). Marking stamps with a postmark also keeps people from reusing them. This post office cancels stamps on about a million letters every day!

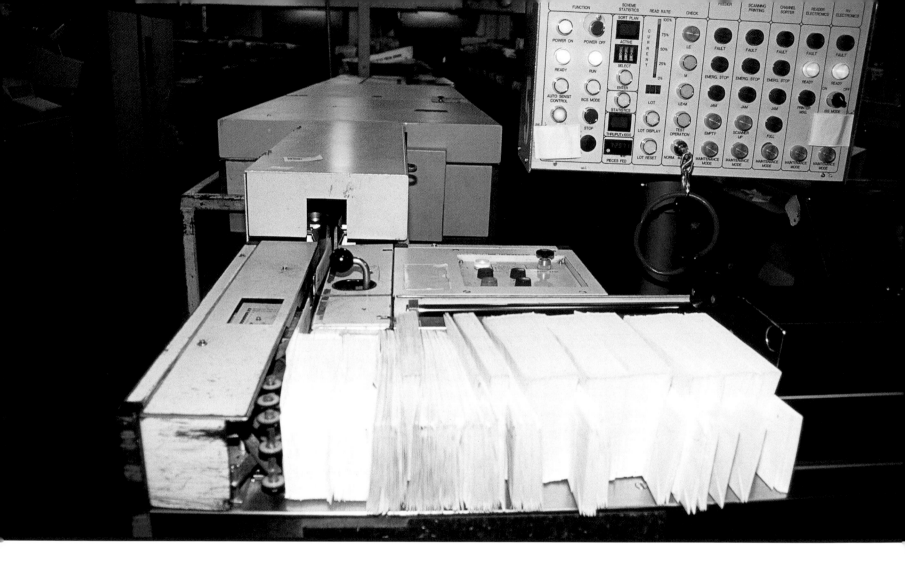

Bar Codes

Next, the letters are fed through a machine called an **Optical Character Reader** (OCR), which automatically reads the address written on the front of the letter.

The OCR translates this information into a **bar code**, a pattern of lines that represent numbers and can be read by other machines. The bar code is printed on the bottom of the front side of each letter.

Bar code

The OCR may not be able to read the addresses on some letters. These are scanned into a computer that sends a picture of the front of the letter to an office where workers "translate" the address. They read the handwriting on the letter and type the address into a computer, which sends the information back to the post office's computer. Then, a bar code can be printed onto the letter.

As technology advances, OCRs will be able to read almost any handwriting, and soon this extra step will no longer be needed.

Sorting

Once the letters have bar codes, they are loaded into a machine called a **Delivery Bar Code Sorter** (DBCS). The DBCS reads the bar codes on the letters and sorts them into different trays depending on which city or town they are going to.

Usually, letters are sorted by **ZIP code** (the five- or nine-digit number at the end of every U.S. address). Some letters may then be sorted by areas or zones within a ZIP code.

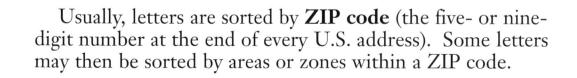

Uncle Steve
5707 West 36th St.
Minneapolis MN 55416

ZIP code

The sorted mail is packed into trays and boxes, which travel by conveyor belt to the post office's shipping area.

Each box of letters is labeled with a computer-printed sticker that has a bar code and letter code on it. This information tells postal workers where the mail is headed. For example, the letter code "BOS" stands for Boston.

Magazines and Catalogs

The post office processes and sorts many other types of mail, including magazines and catalogs. Publishers send magazines and catalogs to the post office in huge shipments. Usually, postal workers sort them by hand.

Packages

The post office also handles packages of all shapes and sizes. After the packages have been separated from other types of mail, hamper dumpers drop them onto the conveyor belts of machines called **Small Parcel Bundle Sorters** (SPBS), as shown at right.

At the top of each conveyor belt, a postal worker sits at a desk with a computer. The workers read the address on each package and type the information into the computer, which then sorts the packages by their destinations.

Each mail container shown below represents a different city or area, and the machine drops the packages into the correct containers.

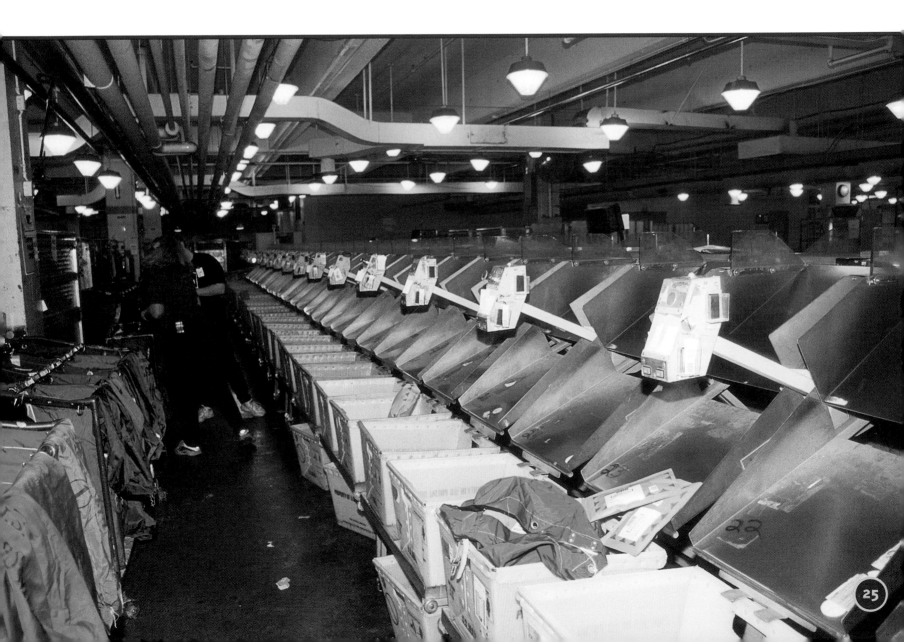

Outgoing Mail

The picture above shows packages that have been packed into bags and are ready to leave the post office. The bags of packages, along with the boxes of letters shown at right, are loaded into trucks. Some trucks will take mail to post offices in nearby cities or towns, or to smaller local post offices within the same city. Mail that is traveling farther away is taken by truck to the airport.

AT 0205/0500
55341   DOOR #39
0205
CHAMPLIN   ELK RIVER

0500
ELK RIVER   CLEAR LAKE
BIG LAKE   CLEARWATER
BECKER

Airplanes

At the airport, the mail is packed into large containers, which are then loaded into airplanes that will carry the mail to another city or country.

Delivery

Once the mail reaches the right city, it is taken to the local post office and sorted into mail carrier routes. Mail carriers, each assigned to a different neighborhood or area of the city, deliver the mail—by truck or on foot—to the correct addresses. Each mail carrier delivers an average of 2,300 pieces of mail every day to about 500 addresses! Whether it's a birthday gift from a faraway relative, a letter from a pen pal, or the newest issue of a favorite magazine, the post office can deliver it all right to your door.

Glossary

Advanced Facer/Canceller: a machine that makes sure all letters are facing the same way and marks (cancels) their postage stamps with a postmark

bar code: a pattern of lines that represent numbers and can be read by machines

conveyor belt: a moving platform that can carry objects from one place to another

Delivery Bar Code Sorter: a machine that reads the bar codes on letters and sorts them by destination

flat extractor: a machine that separates packages, bundles, or thick envelopes from letters

hamper dumper: a machine that picks up containers full of mail and dumps them out

Optical Character Reader: a machine that automatically reads the address on a letter and translates it into a bar code

postmark: a pattern marked onto postage stamps to cancel them, showing the date and the location of the post office

Small Parcel Bundle Sorter: a machine that processes and sorts packages

ZIP code: a five- or nine-digit number at the end of an address that helps the post office sort and deliver mail in the United States